# CONTENTS

Tracking, mixing, and mastering by
Jake Johnson & Bill Maynard at Paradyme Productions
All guitars by Doug Boduch
Bass by Tom McGirr
Drums by Scott Schroedl

ISBN-13: 978-1-4234-0063-9
ISBN-10: 1-4234-0063-1

Visit Hal Leonard Online at **www.halleonard.com**

HAL•LEONARD®
CORPORATION
7777 W. BLUEMOUND RD. P.O. BOX 13819
MILWAUKEE, WISCONSIN 53213

# Am I Evil?

**Words and Music by Sean Harris and Brian Tatler**

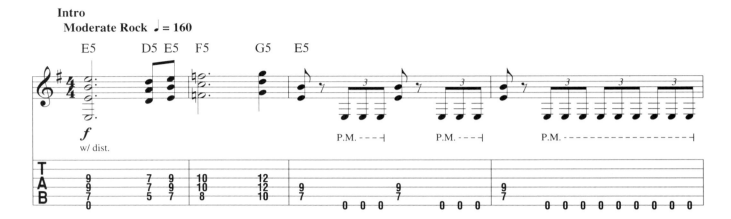

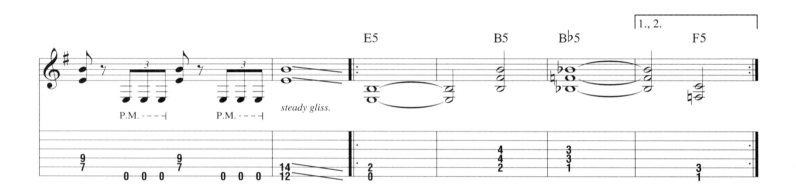

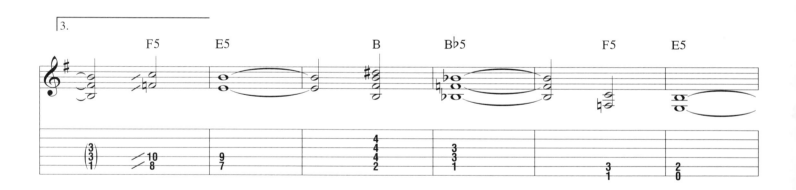

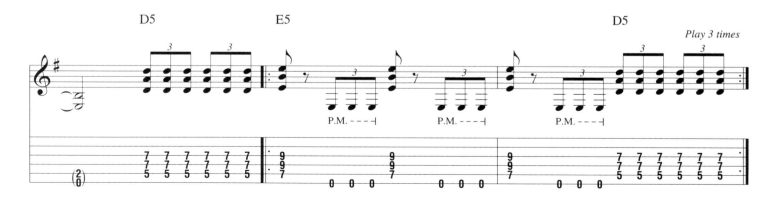

1. My

**Verse**

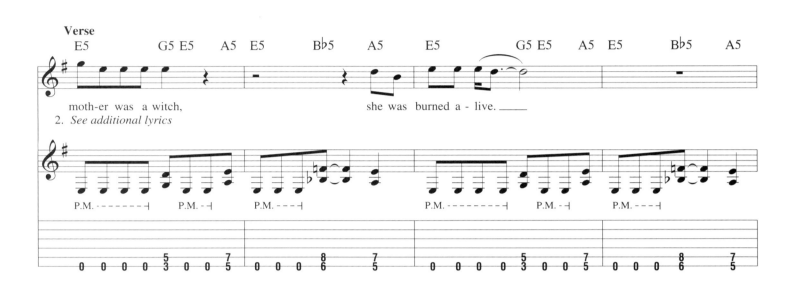

moth-er was a witch, she was burned a - live. _____

2. *See additional lyrics*

**End half-time feel**

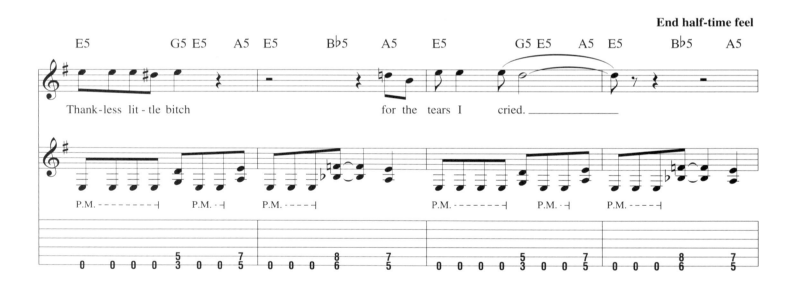

Thank-less lit - tle bitch for the tears I cried. _____

Take her down now, don't want to see her face. _____

All

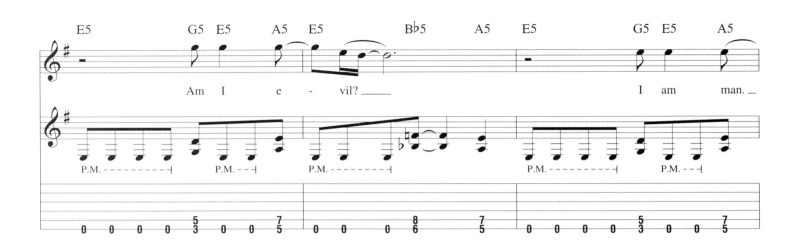

Am I e - vil? _____ I am man. _

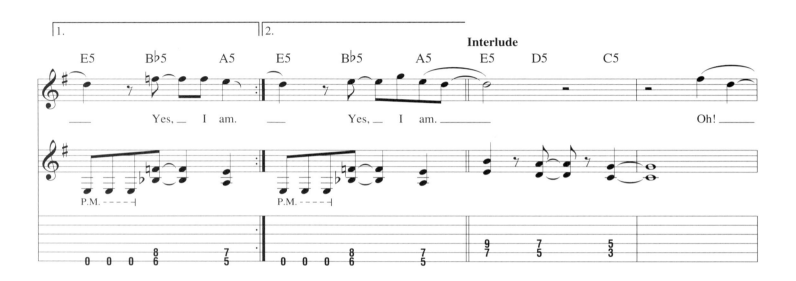

1. | 2. Interlude

_____ Yes, _ I am. _ Yes, _ I am. _____ Oh! _____

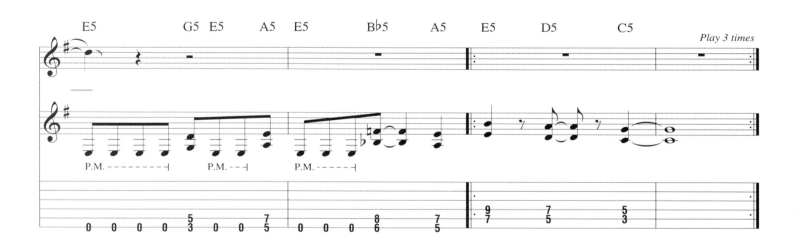

Play 3 times

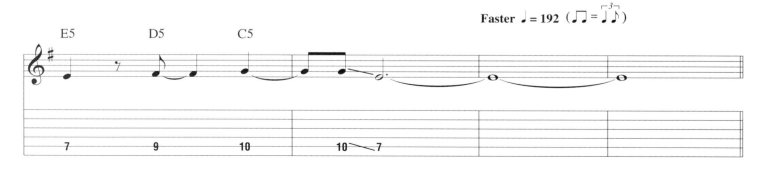

Faster ♩ = 192

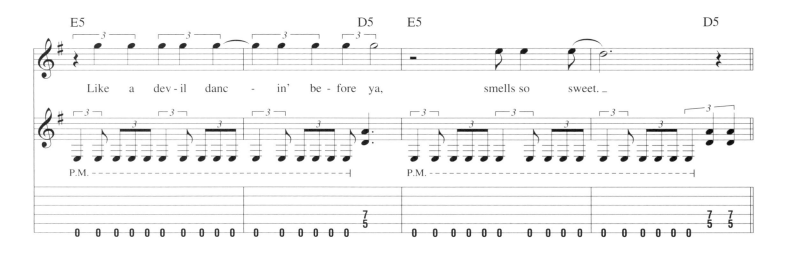

Like a dev - il danc - in' be - fore ya, smells so sweet.

**Chorus**

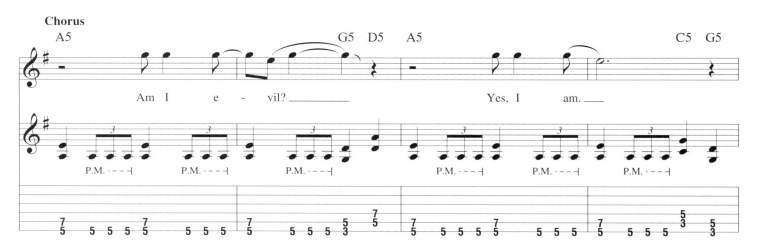

Am I e - vil? Yes, I am.

*3rd time, To Coda*

Am I e - vil? I am man.

**Guitar Solo**

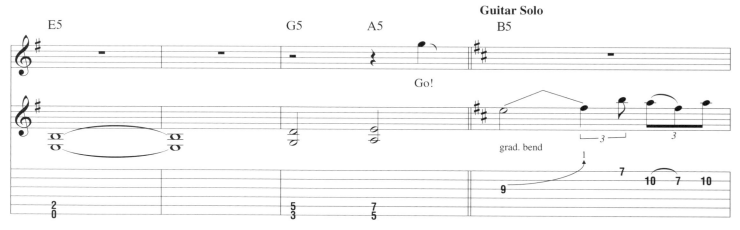

Go!

grad. bend

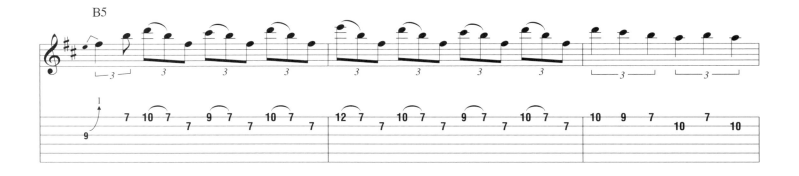

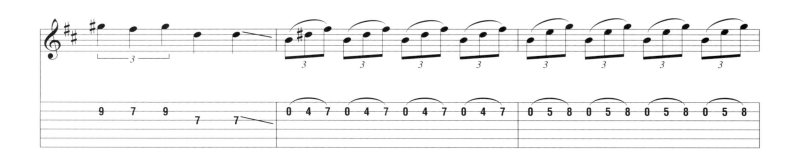

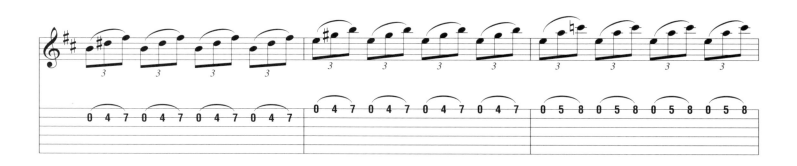

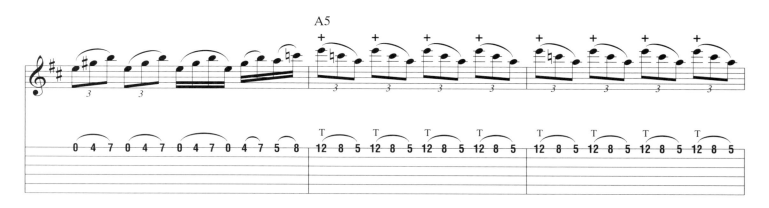

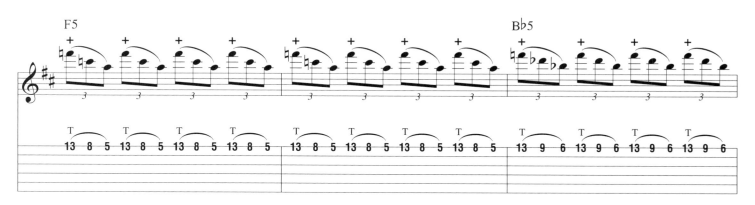

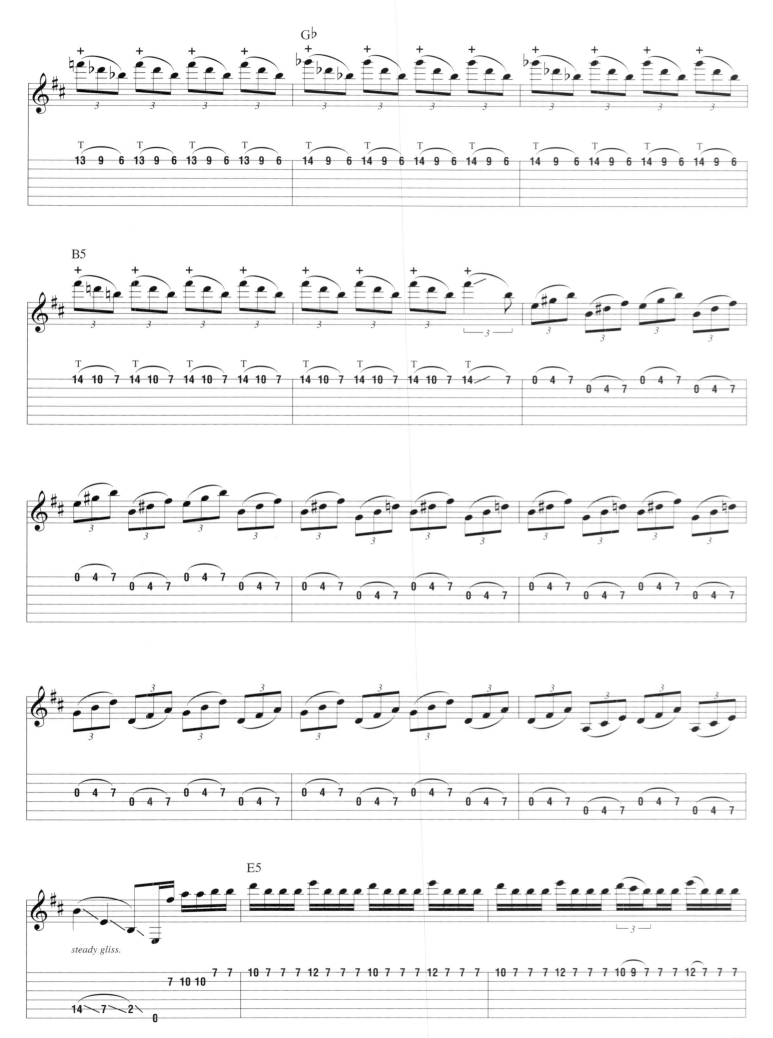

*D.S. al Coda*
*(take repeat)*

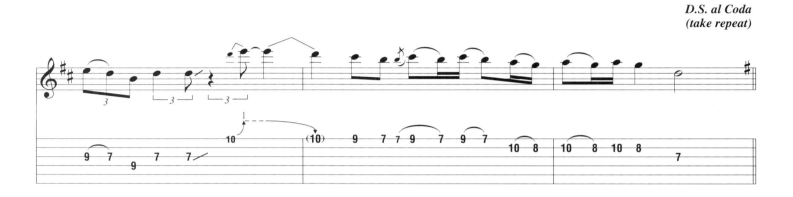

**Coda**

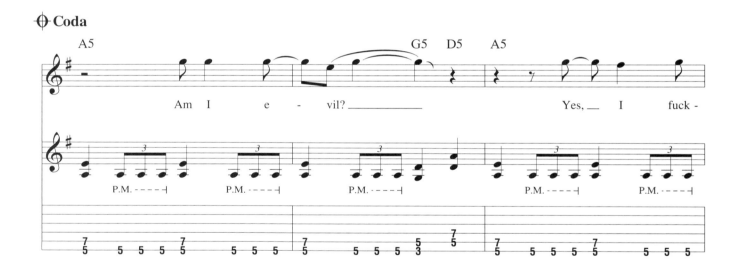

Am I e - vil? _____ Yes, __ I fuck -

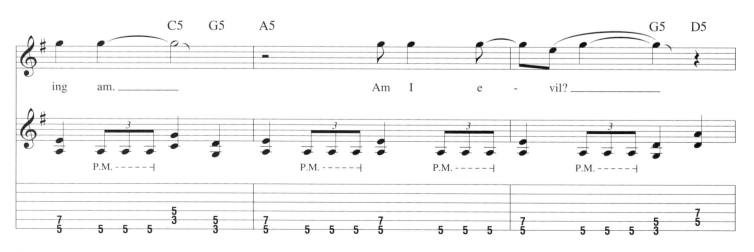

ing am. _____ Am I e - vil? _____

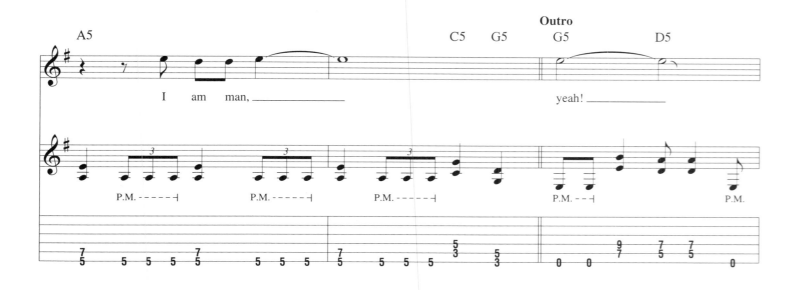

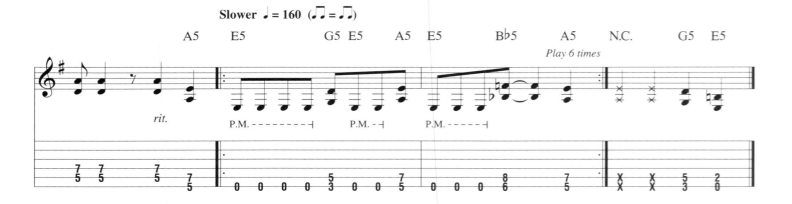

*Additional Lyrics*

2. As I watched my mother die, I lost my head.
Revenge now I sought to break with my bread.
Takin' no chances, you come with me.
I'll split you to the bone, help set you free.

*Bridge* 2. I'll make my residence, I'll watch your fire.
You can come with me, sweet desire.
My face is long forgotten, my face not my own.
Sweet and timely whore, take me home.

*Bridge* 3. My soul is longing for, await my hell,
Set to avenge my mother, sweeten myself.
My face is long forgotten, my face not my own.
Sweet and timely whore, take me home.

# Back in Black

Words and Music by Angus Young, Malcolm Young and Brian Johnson

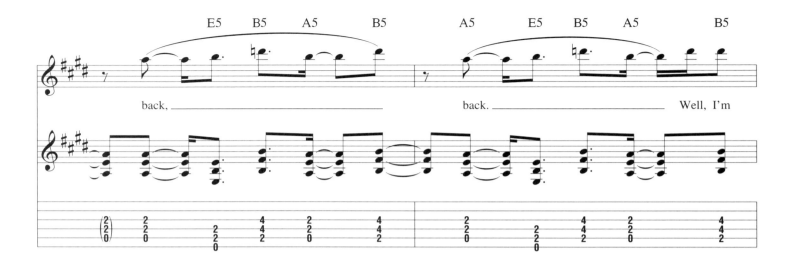

E5   B5   A5       B5        A5    E5   B5   A5            B5

back, _____  back. _____  Well, I'm

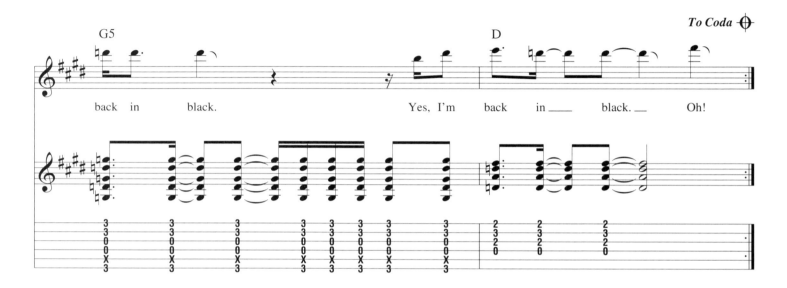

*To Coda* ⊕

G5                                    D

back   in   black.        Yes, I'm   back   in ____   black. ___   Oh!

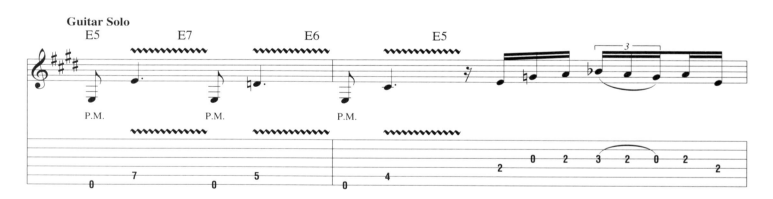

**Guitar Solo**

E5      E7        E6        E5

P.M.        P.M.        P.M.

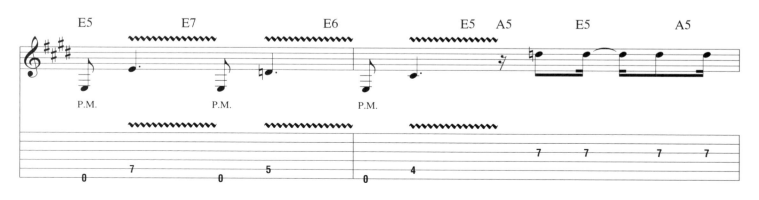

E5      E7        E6        E5    A5    E5        A5

P.M.        P.M.        P.M.

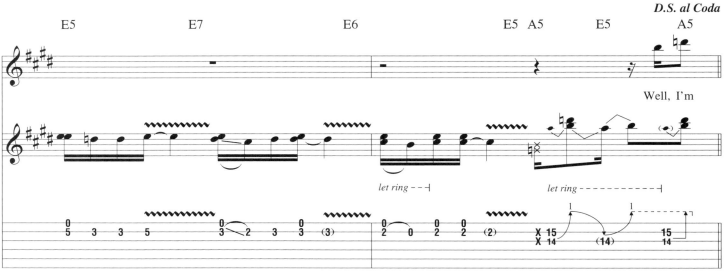

Well, I'm

## ⊕ Coda

**Interlude**

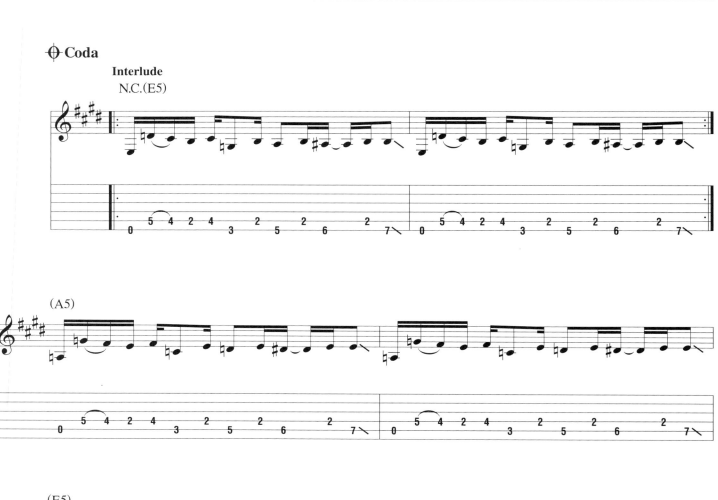

Well, I'm

**Outro-Guitar Solo**

*Additional Lyrics*

2. Back in the back of a Cadillac.
   Number one with a bullet, I'm a power pack.
   Yes, I'm in the band, with the gang.
   They got to catch me if they want me to hang
   'Cause I'm back on the track,
   And I'm beatin' the flack.
   Nobody's gonna get me on another rap.
   So look at me now, I'm just a makin' my pay.
   Don't try to push your luck, just get outta my way.

# You've Got Another Thing Comin'

Words and Music by Glenn Tipton, Rob Halford and K.K. Downing

never get e-nough.                                                    Stand _

_ tall. ____     I'm ___  a  young  and  kind  of  proud.

I'm  on   the  top,   but  as  long ___   as  the  mu-sic's   loud. _

**Pre-Chorus**
F#5                                                                    D5

1., 3. If   you  think  I'll    sit   a - round ___  as _
2. *See additional lyrics*

the world goes by, you're think-in' like a fool 'cause it's a case __ of do or die. __ Out __

there is a for-tune wait - ing to be had. __ If you think I'll let it go you're mad. __

Chorus

You've got an-oth-er thing com-in'. You've got an-oth-er thing

com - in'. 2. That's __ com - in'.

To Coda ⊕

Bridge

24

Guitar Solo

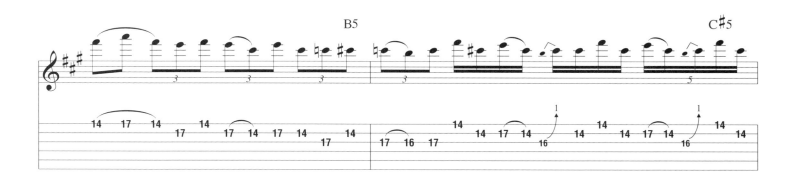

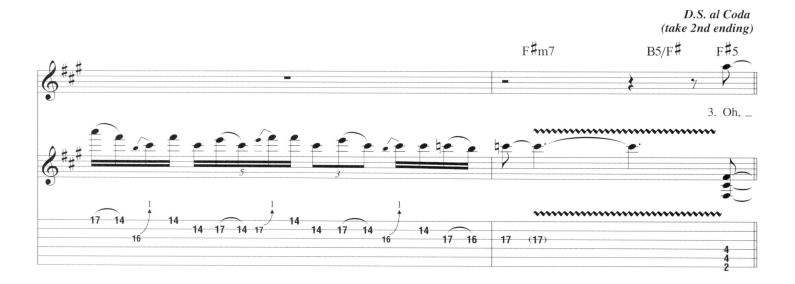

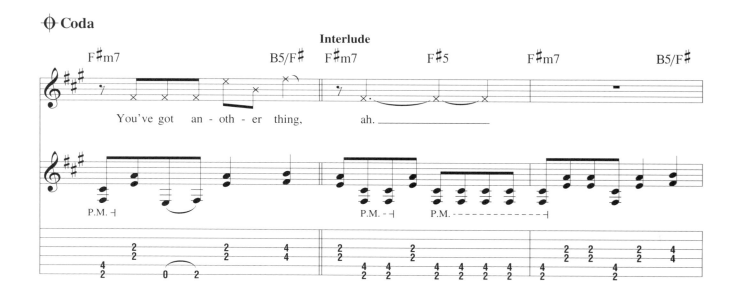

*Play 10 times and fade*

**Outro**

Com - in' on down!

You've got an - oth - er thing com - in'.

*Additional Lyrics*

2. That's right, here's where the talking ends.
   Well listen, this night there'll be some action spent.
   Drive hard. Callin' all the shots.
   I got an ace card comin' down the rocks.

*Pre-Chorus* 2. If you think I'll sit around while you chip away my brain,
   Listen, I ain't foolin' and you'd better think again.
   Out there is a fortune waiting to be had.
   If you think I'll let it go you're mad.

3. Oh, so hot. No time to take a rest, yeah.
   Act tough, ain't room for second best.
   Real strong. Got me some security.
   Hey, I'm a big smash; I'm goin' for infinity, yeah.

# Holy Diver

**Words and Music by Ronnie James Dio**

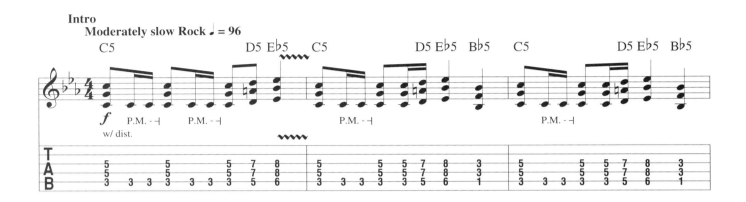

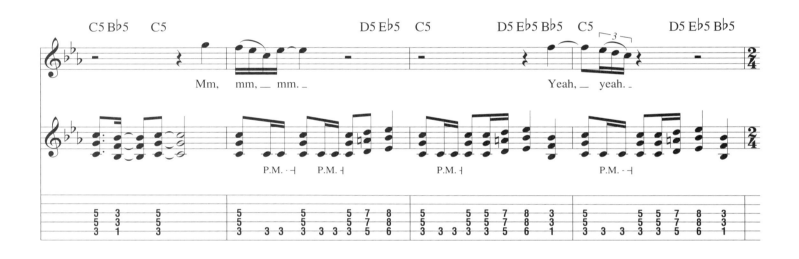

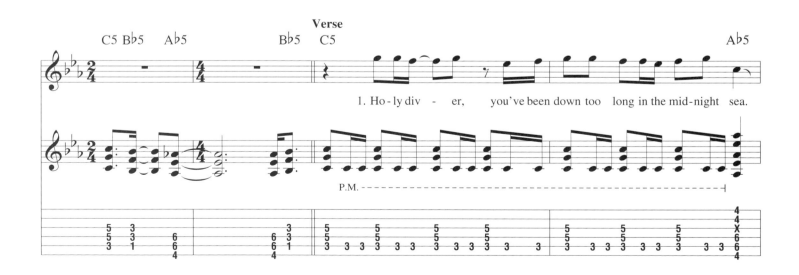

## %  Verse

2nd time, substitute Fill 1

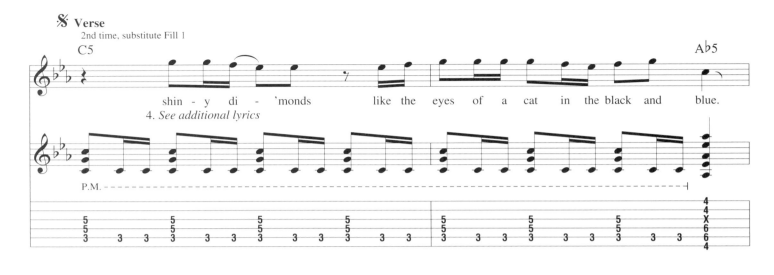

shin - y di - 'monds like the eyes of a cat in the black and blue.

4. *See additional lyrics*

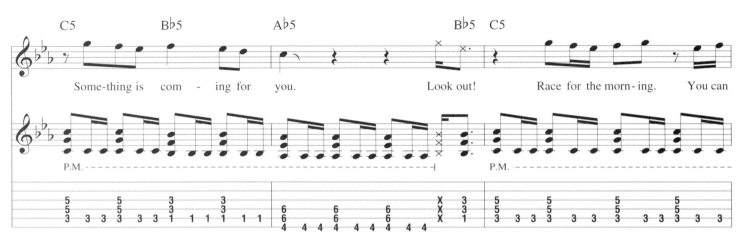

Some-thing is com - ing for you. Look out! Race for the morn-ing. You can

hide in the sun till you see the light. Oh, we will pray it's al - right.

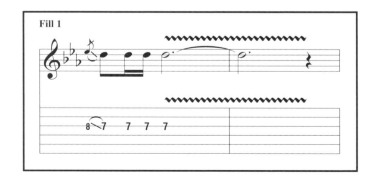

**Fill 1**

# Lights Out

### Words and Music by Michael Schenker, Phil Mogg, Andy Parker and Pete Way

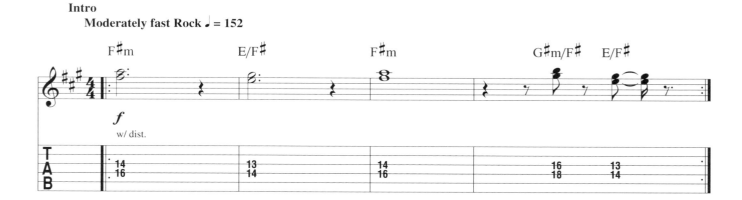

1. Wind blows_ back_ and _ the bat-tle's_ charg-in', _ it winds all the way._
2. *See additional lyrics*

*Chord symbols reflect overall harmony.

Up to _ the butt of my _ gun. _____

§ Chorus
2nd time, substitute Fill 1

Fill 1

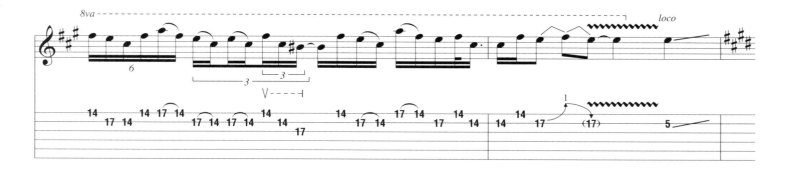

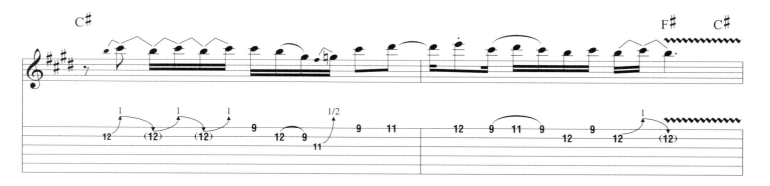

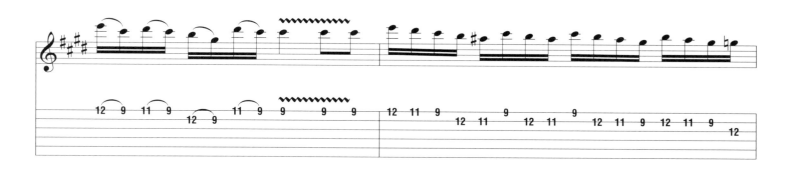

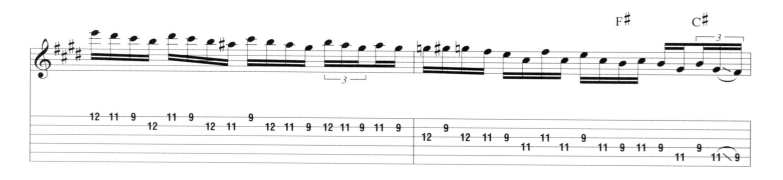

43

**Outro-Guitar Solo**

Lights out, lights __ out __ in Lon - don.

Pitch: D♯

*Begin fade*

Lights out, lights _____ out _____ in Lon - don.

*Additional Lyrics*

2. From the back streets
   There's a rumblin';
   Smell of anarchy.
   No more nice time,
   Bright boy shoe shines;
   Pie-in-the-sky dreams.

4. You keep comin',
   There's no runnin';
   Tried a thousand times.
   Under your feet,
   Grass is growin'.
   Time we said goodbye.

# The Trooper

**Words and Music by Steven Harris**

Intro
Moderately fast Rock ♩ = 160

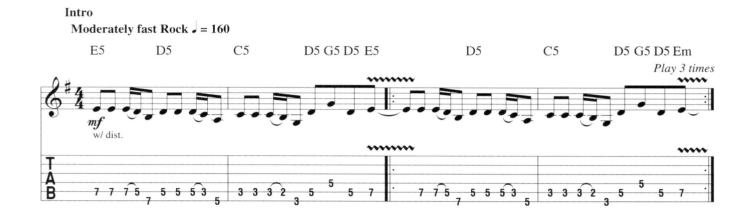

2nd time, substitute Fill 1

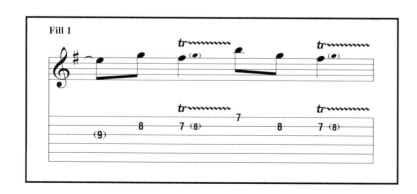

The smell of ac- rid smoke and hors- es' breath __

as I plunge on in- to cer- tain death.

Oh. __

**%** **Chorus**

2nd time, substitute Fill 2

**Fill 2**

We won't live to fight an - oth - er day. Oh.

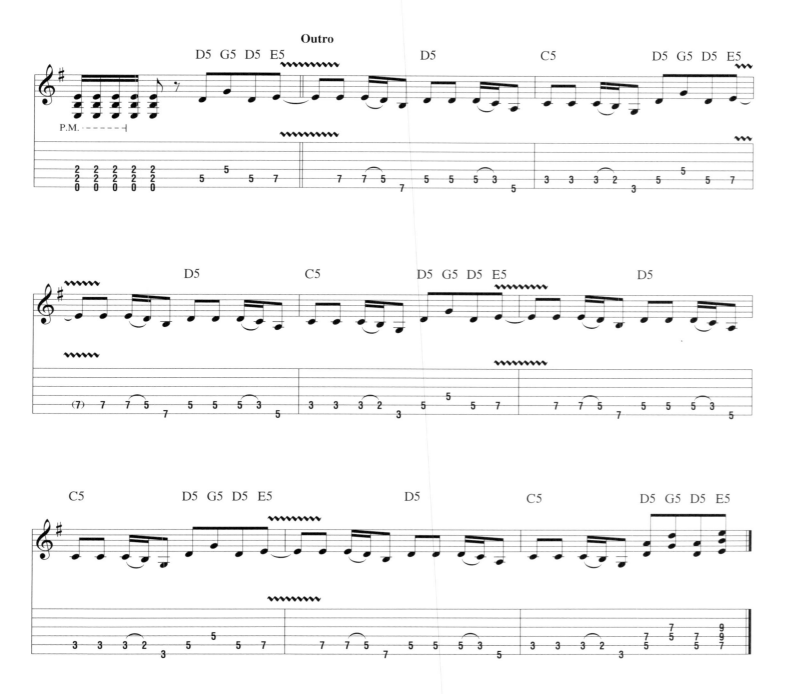

*Additional Lyrics*

3. We get so close, near enough to fight,
   When a Russian gets me in his sights.
   He pulls the trigger and I feel the blow,
   A burst of rounds takes my horse below.
   And as I lay there gazing at the sky,
   My body's numb and my throut is dry.
   And as I lay forgotten and alone,
   Without a tear I draw my parting groan.

# The Zoo

Words and Music by Klaus Meine and Rudolf Schenker

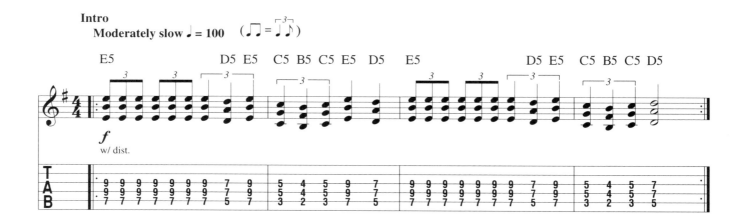

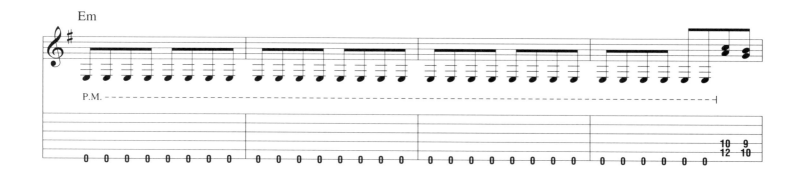

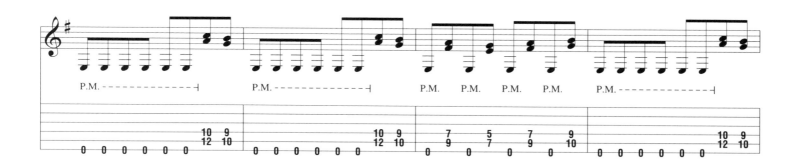

§ **Verse**

Em

1. The job is done, __ I go out, __ an-
2., 3. *See additional lyrics*

3rd time, substitute Fill 1

oth - er bor - ing day. __ I leave it all _____ be -

**Fill 1**

*8va*

grad. bend
w/ talk box

1 1/2

21

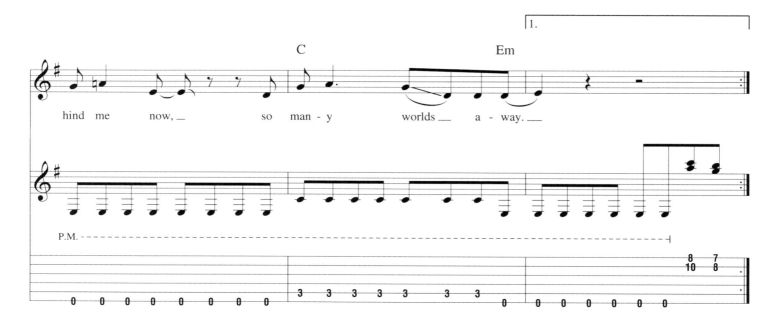

hind me now, __ so man - y worlds __ a - way. __

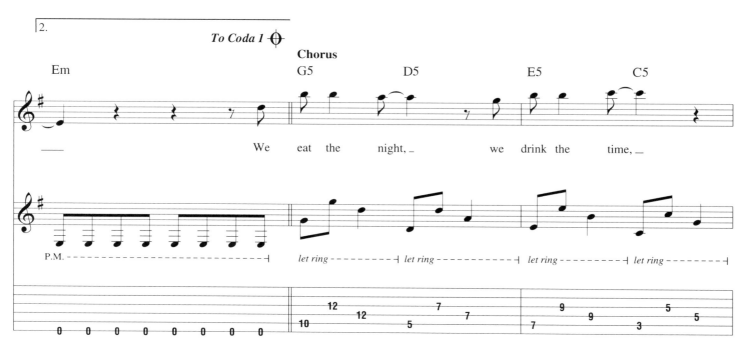

We eat the night, __ we drink the time, __

make our dreams __ come true. __ And hun - gry eyes __ are

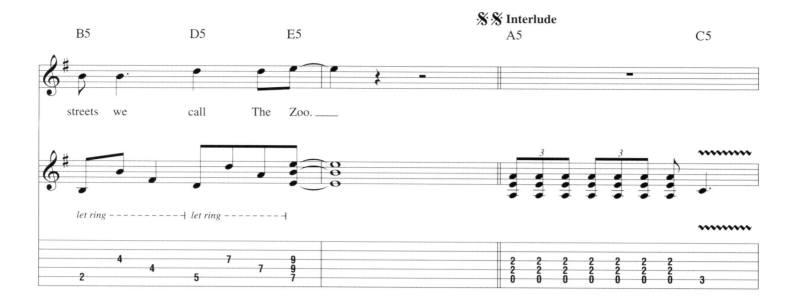

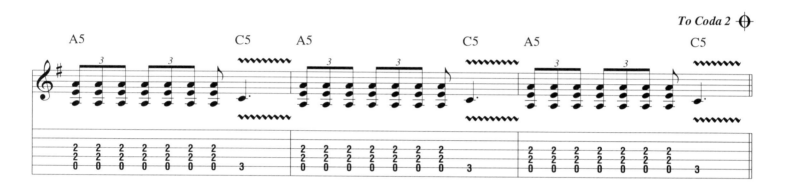

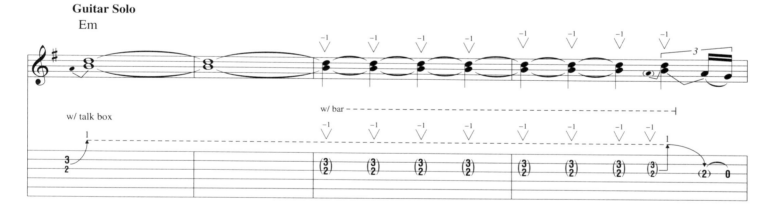

drink the    time, ___          make our    dreams ___ come    true. ___

And    hun - gry    eyes ___        are

*D.S.S. al Coda 2*

pass - ing    by ___        on    streets we    call    The    Zoo. _____

### Coda 2
**Outro-Guitar Solo**
Em

w/ talk box
grad. bend

62

**Additional Lyrics**

2. I meet my girl, she's dressed to kill.
   But all we gonna do
   Is walk around to catch the thrill
   On streets we call The Zoo.

3. Enjoy The Zoo and walk down
   42nd Street.
   Wanna be excited too,
   And you will feel the heat.

# Guitar Notation Legend

**THE MUSICAL STAFF** shows pitches and rhythms and is divided by bar lines into measures. Pitches are named after the first seven letters of the alphabet.

**TABLATURE** graphically represents the guitar fingerboard. Each horizontal line represents a string, and each number represents a fret.

4th string, 2nd fret      1st & 2nd strings open, played together     open D chord

**HALF-STEP BEND:** Strike the note and bend up 1/2 step.

**WHOLE-STEP BEND:** Strike the note and bend up one step.

**GRACE NOTE BEND:** Strike the note and bend up as indicated. The first note does not take up any time.

**SLIGHT (MICROTONE) BEND:** Strike the note and bend up 1/4 step.

**BEND AND RELEASE:** Strike the note and bend up as indicated, then release back to the original note. Only the first note is struck.

**PRE-BEND:** Bend the note as indicated, then strike it.

**VIBRATO:** The string is vibrated by rapidly bending and releasing the note with the fretting hand.

**PALM MUTING:** The note is partially muted by the pick hand lightly touching the string(s) just before the bridge.

**HAMMER-ON:** Strike the first (lower) note with one finger, then sound the higher note (on the same string) with another finger by fretting it without picking.

**PULL-OFF:** Place both fingers on the notes to be sounded. Strike the first note and without picking, pull the finger off to sound the second (lower) note.

**LEGATO SLIDE:** Strike the first note and then slide the same fret-hand finger up or down to the second note. The second note is not struck.

**SHIFT SLIDE:** Same as legato slide, except the second note is struck.

**TRILL:** Very rapidly alternate between the notes indicated by continuously hammering on and pulling off.

**TAPPING:** Hammer ("tap") the fret indicated with the pick-hand index or middle finger and pull off to the note fretted by the fret hand.

**NATURAL HARMONIC:** Strike the note while the fret-hand lightly touches the string directly over the fret indicated.

**PINCH HARMONIC:** The note is fretted normally and a harmonic is produced by adding the edge of the thumb or the tip of the index finger of the pick hand to the normal pick attack.

**TREMOLO PICKING:** The note is picked as rapidly and continuously as possible.

**VIBRATO BAR DIVE AND RETURN:** The pitch of the note or chord is dropped a specified number of steps (in rhythm) then returned to the original pitch.

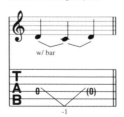

**VIBRATO BAR SCOOP:** Depress the bar just before striking the note, then quickly release the bar.

**VIBRATO BAR DIP:** Strike the note and then immediately drop a specified number of steps, then release back to the original pitch.

# Additional Musical Definitions

 *(accent)*   • Accentuate note (play it louder)

 *(staccato)*   • Play the note short

**D.S. al Coda**   • Go back to the sign (𝄋), then play until the measure marked *"To Coda"*, then skip to the section labelled *"Coda."*

**D.C. al Fine**   • Go back to the beginning of the song and play until the measure marked *"Fine"* (end).

**Fill**   • Label used to identify a brief melodic figure which is to be inserted into the arrangement.

**N.C.**   • Instrument is silent (drops out).

   • Repeat measures between signs.

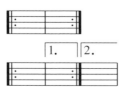   • When a repeated section has different endings, play the first ending only the first time and the second ending only the second time.